Nelson

ENGLISH
SKILLS
BOOK 4

JOHN JACKMAN
WENDY WREN

Nelson

Contents

Vocabulary	Punctuation/ Grammar	Spelling	Quiz
'would' and 'should'	capital letters abstract nouns	singular and plural nouns	collective nouns
onomatopoeia	ending sentences pronouns	'l' and 'll'	'able' endings
French words in English	capital letters in titles adverbs (comparative)	words from French	French cities and towns
homonyms and homophones	conversations irregular verbs	silent letters	word games
foreign words synonyms	prepositions using: is/are/was/were	'sure' endings	anagrams
'may' and 'can' prefixes 're' and 'ex'	adjectives and adverbs phrases	'ss' with 'ion'	word game
dictionary work idioms	verbs (active and passive)	double consonants	hidden words
contractions	double negatives	silent 'h'	punctuation puzzle
'among' and 'between' hyphens and compound words	divided direct speech using 'did' and 'done'	'ance' or 'ence'?	missing letters
proverbs	spoken English standard English	'gue' endings	dialect quiz
interjections	conversations phrases and clauses	'ckle' pattern	spoonerisms
hyperbole	hyphens at line-breaks main clauses	'ious' or 'ous'	word pyramid
unnecessary words	business letters	'augh' pattern	map of Bangladesh

Grace Darling

It was a dark, windy night in 1838. An old Scottish paddle-steamer, the *Forfarshire*, was on a voyage from Hull to Dundee. Although Captain Humble knew that one of his ship's boilers was leaking he didn't think it was too serious, but as the storm began to blow up and the wind and waves grew, both engines suddenly stopped. The ship began drifting helplessly. Knowing that they were in dire trouble, the captain and crew became frightened for their lives.

Captain Humble tried to comfort and encourage everyone, as he had seen a light which he assumed was shining on the island of Inner Farne. What he didn't realise was that it was not Inner Farne but the Longstone lighthouse, there to warn shipping of the treacherous rocks! Suddenly, with a terrifying lurch, the *Forfarshire* struck the Big Hancar rocks. Almost immediately, under the pounding of the raging storm, the vessel began to break up.

By the end of that long and terrible night only nine survivors, including Captain Humble and his wife, remained clinging to the rocks. Shivering and frightened as the huge waves crashed over them, they knew they could not hold out much longer. Any moment one of those huge waves would drag them into that ferocious sea.

As daybreak came, the lighthouse keeper's daughter woke and looked out from her window. In the distance she saw shapes on a rock which she thought were seals, quite common in those waters. Then suddenly, as the light became slowly brighter, she realised with horror that they were not seals, but human beings!

The sea was still very rough – far too rough for Mr Darling, the lighthouse keeper, to row his boat across. It would have been impossible for one person, strong though he was. "But we can't just leave them to drown," pleaded Grace. "If we both go, we can row together."

At first Mr Darling dismissed the very thought of allowing Grace anywhere near that treacherous sea, but Grace was not to be put off. She couldn't stand by and watch those desperate people swept from the rocks. She was determined that something had to be done!

It will never be known how the two felt as they struggled to launch their small boat into those huge waves and gale-force winds, but we do know that the storm was so bad it nearly sank their flimsy vessel before it reached the rocks. However, once they had started, Grace and Mr Darling knew that they could not abandon their rescue attempt and leave the nine to be swept to their deaths. Straining every muscle, and with little thought for their own survival, they fought and struggled their way through the mountainous waves.

The rowing boat was too small to rescue all nine survivors, so having transferred the first group to the lighthouse, Grace and her father set off again, not satisfied until all nine were safe inside the lighthouse.

Grace Darling and her father became national heroes, praised throughout the country for their great bravery, and are remembered to this day for being prepared to selflessly risk their own lives in order to save others.

A Copy these sentences, filling in the missing words.

1 The *Forfarshire* was sailing to ____ .

2 She struck the ____ ____ rocks.

3 The paddle-steamer soon broke up in the ____ storm.

4 The survivors were ____ and ____ as they waited to be rescued.

B Write sentences to answer each question.

1 Who was the keeper of the Longstone lighthouse?

2 Why did he think he would not be able to rescue the stranded survivors?

3 What words are used to describe how the crew of the *Forfarshire* felt on that terrible night? Add three more of your own that the writer might have used to describe their feelings.

4 How would you have felt and what would you have done if you had been in Grace's position?

VOCABULARY

Using 'should' and 'would'

We usually write:
- **should** after 'I' and 'we'
- **would** after 'you', 'they', 'he', 'she' and 'it'.

If we want to make a strong statement, we reverse this rule:
- **should** after 'you', 'they', 'he', 'she' and 'it'
- **would** after 'I' and 'we'.

Examples: I **should** like to visit a lighthouse.
I **would** not like to be shipwrecked!

A Copy these sentences, filling in the gaps with **should** or **would**.

1 I ____ not like to be stranded on a rock.

2 It ____ be very frightening.

3 You ____ need to be extremely brave to work on a lifeboat.

4 The lady asked if we ____ like to go for a ride on a lifeboat.

5 We said that we ____ like to, very much!

B Write two sentences of your own, one using **should** and the other using **would**.

PUNCTUATION

Using capital letters

Capital letters are used to begin sentences, and for these types of word:

People's titles, initials and names	*Captain Humble, Miss G Darling*
Buildings	*St Paul's Cathedral*
Places	*Hull, Dundee*
Names of ships and aircraft	*HMS Ark Royal*
Adjectives made from names	*Scottish, American*
Streets	*High Street, North Road*
Days and months	*Tuesday, October*
Important words in book titles etc	*Rescue on the Rocks*
Names of companies	*Cunard Shipping Company*
'I' by itself	*I*

A Write these groups of words. Some of the words should begin with capital letters. Put capital letters where they are needed.

1 mrs eve stephens, teacher, caversham primary school

2 queen elizabeth, city, buckingham palace, london

3 australia, melbourne, kangaroos, sydney opera house

4 monday, february, i, we, the koran, the bible

B Write this passage, adding the missing capital letters. Look at the box above to give you some clues.

it was monday, and mrs lindsay's class was taking assembly. they acted out a play about grace darling and how she and mr darling had saved captain humble and the crew of the *forfarshire* after it struck the big hancar rocks, near the longstone lighthouse. afterwards i found the story in a book called great deeds of courage.

A **proper noun** is a *special* name word, and it has a capital letter.

Remember, **nouns** are 'name' words.
There are several types of **noun**.
Most nouns are names for things you can see and touch.
These are **common nouns** and **proper nouns**.
Examples: ship   lighthouse   Grace

You can't see, touch, taste, smell or hear the things that are named by **abstract nouns**. They are the names of qualities, feelings, times or actions.
Examples: courage   night   Monday

A   Write a list of eight nouns which are things you could touch in each of these places. Include at least two proper nouns.

1   At the seaside

2   On a ship

B   Write a list of eight **abstract** nouns, which are things you can't see, touch, taste, smell or hear. Include at least one proper noun.

C   Put four of the words you have listed into interesting sentences to show that you understand what each of them means.

Remember, to make a noun plural we usually either:

- add **s** (ship, ship**s**)
- add **es**, if it ends in **ch**, **sh**, **s** or **x**
  (wat**ch**, watch**es**; box, box**es**)
- change the **y** to **i** and add **es**, if it ends in a **consonant** and a **y**
  (c**ry**, cr**ies**)

A Write the plural form of each of these nouns.

1 night	2 sailor	3 church	4 sky	5 dish
6 navy	7 fly	8 bush	9 daughter	10 fox

Match a **collective noun** from the box to each of these groups of creatures. The first one is done to help you. **A** = a litter of kittens

herd	litter	flock	pride
school	gaggle	shoal	

Fishing

This paragraph by the American writer Ernest Hemingway is about an old man out in his boat who has just hooked a very large fish.

He could not see by the slant of the line that the fish was circling. It was too early for that. He just felt a faint slackening of the pressure of the line and he commenced to pull on it gently with his right hand. It tightened, as always, but just when he reached the point where it would break, line began to come in. He slipped his shoulders and head from under the line and began to pull in line steadily and gently. He used both of his hands in a swinging motion and tried to do the pulling as much as he could with his body and his legs. His old legs and shoulders pivoted with the swinging of the pulling.

From *The Old Man and the Sea* by Ernest Hemingway.

COMPREHENSION

Remember, an adjective is a 'describing' word.

A   Copy these sentences, filling in the missing words.

1   The fisherman could not see that the ＿＿ was circling.

2   The old man pulled the line ＿＿ and ＿＿ .

3   He used his hands in a ＿＿ motion.

B   Write sentences to answer these questions.

1   How do we know that the fish the old man had hooked was big?

2   Write at least four adjectives that might describe the old man's feelings as he struggled with the fish.

The Silver Fish

While fishing in the blue lagoon
I caught a lovely silver fish,
And he spoke to me, "My boy," quoth he,
"Please set me free and I'll grant your wish . . .
A kingdom of wisdom? A palace of gold?
Or all the goodies your mind can hold?"
So I said, "OK," and I threw him free,
And he swam away and he laughed at me
Whispering my foolish wish
Into a silent sea.
Today I caught that fish again,
That lovely silver prince of fishes
And once again he offered me—
If I would only set him free—
Any one of a number of wonderful wishes . . .
He was delicious!

Shel Silverstein

COMPREHENSION

A Copy these sentences, filling in the missing words.

1 The boy was fishing in a ____ lagoon.

2 The fish promised to grant the boy a ____ .

3 In the end the boy ____ the fish.

B Write sentences to answer these questions about the poem.

1 What did the silver fish promise the boy if he set him free?

2 Do you think that the boy was cruel to eat the fish?
   Give reasons for your answer.

Remember, a word which sounds like the noise it describes is an **onomatopoeic** or 'sound' word. Can you see why this poem by Max Dunn is called *The Onomatopoeia River*?

Glade . . . shade . . . pool . . . cool . . .
Fickle trickle . . . supple . . . able . . .
Yearning . . . trending . . . wending.

(Read each line faster.)

Amble, addle, dawdle, dabble,
babble, bubble, gurgle, gambol,
bustle hustle tussle tumble,
mumble-grumble-rumble, hurtle-
Lunge! Plunge!
Splash! Spray,
flay, fume.
Gnash! Lash! Rage, wage.

(Read each line slower.)

Freed, speed . . .
weed . . . reed . . .
haze . . . laze . . .
hide . . . glide . . .
wide . . . tide.

A List six of the most descriptive onomatopoeic words in this poem.

B Choose a noisy situation, such as a firework party or busy traffic in a town, and describe it. Each sentence must contain at least one onomatopoeic word.

PUNCTUATION

Ending sentences

There are three punctuation marks which can be used to end a sentence – a full stop (.), a question mark (?) or an exclamation mark (!).

A Copy these sentences, adding the correct punctuation mark at the end of each one.

1 I always enjoy a day's fishing, don't you

2 Did Dean catch anything yesterday

3 He caught one absolutely huge one

4 How much did it weigh

5 I don't know, he put it straight back

6 He's crazy

GRAMMAR

Pronouns

Remember, 'pro' at the beginning of a word sometimes means 'in place of'.

Pronouns are used in place of nouns.
Examples: **I, you, she, her, it, we, us, they, them**

A **possessive pronoun** is a pronoun that shows who or what owns something.
Examples:
The fishing rod is **mine/yours/his/hers/ours/theirs**.

A Read the paragraph and poem on pages 10 and 11 again. Write their titles, and next to each, make a list of any pronouns you can find.

B Write these sentences, using the correct **possessive pronoun** from the box above in place of the words in brackets.

1 Her sister said she would lend me (her rod).

2 I thought (her rod) was better than (my rod).

3 May I share (your rod)?

4 I sometimes forget which is (her gear) and which is (my gear).

SPELLING

'l' and 'll'

Usually **ll** patterns are found in the middle of words.
It is usual to have one **l** at the end of words.
Example: beautifu**l**
beautifu**lly**

Complete each word with **l** or **ll**. Check your answers in a dictionary.

1 fue __	2 unti __	3 spoonfu __	4 wonderfu __
5 umbre __ a	6 leve __	7 crue __ y	8 tota __
9 a __ ow	10 grow __	11 wou __ d	12 beautifu __

QUIZ

Fishing expedition

For every word you can complete with **able**, you catch a fish.
Make one list of the fish that you catch, and another list of those that are left in the pond. Check your answers in a dictionary.

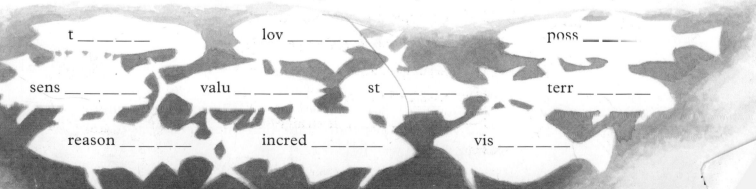

t _ _ _ _ _   lov _ _ _ _ _   poss _ _ _

sens _ _ _ _ _   valu _ _ _ _ _   st _ _ _ _ _   terr _ _ _ _ _

reason _ _ _ _ _   incred _ _ _ _ _   vis _ _ _ _ _

France – heroes of fiction

The French have many different heroes both in legend and in fiction. Some of these are international, such as Robin Hood and Superman, but many are French heroes, not always so well known in other countries. Some, such as Captain Nemo, Guignol and Quasimodo, have been popular for generations; others, like Asterix the Gaul, are newer. Asterix is now famous throughout the world and enjoyed by both children and adults alike.

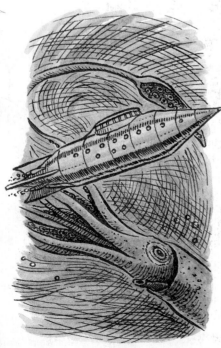

Two of the most famous French writers of adventure stories are Jules Verne, who used scientific settings and plots, and Alexandre Dumas, who wrote about historical events.

Jules Verne was born in Nantes in 1828 and, incredibly, although he wrote more than 100 years ago, many of his predictions have come true, which is one of the reasons why so many readers still find his stories so fascinating. In one of his books he imagines his characters being able to fly to the moon in a rocket, something which must have seemed a ridiculous proposition in the 1860s. Jules Verne's most popular and best-known books are *Twenty Thousand Leagues under the Sea* and *Around the World in Eighty Days*.

This scene is from *Twenty Thousand Leagues under the Sea*, in which the hero, Captain Nemo (Nemo is Latin for 'nobody'!), has many adventures in his submarine *Nautilus*, which could perform some manoeuvres which weren't possible in real life for another hundred years. Many people think that Jules Verne was the 'father' of science fiction writing.

Dumas was a prodigious writer. It is said that in one year (1844) he actually had 44 books published! Probably his most famous is *The Three Musketeers*, one of those published in that year. The following year another well-known book, *The Man in the Iron Mask*, was published. Dumas's books were mostly historical fiction. These are loosely based on historical facts, but the author adds many extra events to ensure it makes a good story.

The Man in the Iron Mask was a real prisoner who was kept for over 40 years in the Bastille prison. In this novel, Dumas imagines that the man in the mask was the twin brother of the king, Louis XIV; but we shall never know whether this was true, as his identity remains a mystery to this day.

These novels by Verne and Dumas have been made into famous films and television series.

D'Artagnan and the Musketeers battling with soldiers sent by the scheming Cardinal de Richelieu. In this story, which was originally written as a newspaper serial, the Musketeers see and manage to prevent many unfortunate events in history.

COMPREHENSION

A Copy these sentences, filling in the missing words.

1 ____ and ____ are both famous French authors.

2 Captain Nemo's submarine was called ____ .

3 *The Three Musketeers* was Alexandre Dumas's most ____ book.

4 Dumas was a ____ writer.

B Write sentences to answer these questions.

1 Why is Jules Verne said to be the 'father' of science fiction?

2 Without looking in a dictionary, say what the writer means by 'Dumas was a prodigious writer.'

3 What is 'historical fiction'?

4 Why is Asterix especially popular in France?

VOCABULARY

French words in English

At different times in the last 1000 years French has been the main language spoken by kings and queens of England and their courtiers, so it is not surprising that many English words have grown out of French words.
Examples: libre – liberty
nom – name

A Here are some French words. Can you think which English words are their near relations? The pictures will give you a clue.

1 vin   2 chambre   3 langue

4 chandelle   5 lune   6 brun

B Check your answers in a French/English dictionary.

PUNCTUATION

Capital letters in titles

> Capital letters should be used for the first letter of the first word and other **important** words in titles.
>
> *Examples:* **A**round the **W**orld in **E**ighty **D**ays
>
> **T**he **M**an in the **I**ron **M**ask
>
> Notice that **articles** (a, an, the) and **short prepositions** (in, on, etc) don't usually need capitals.

A Write these titles, putting in the capital letters.

1 the three musketeers

2 asterix the gaul

3 the lion, the witch and the wardrobe

4 the little house on the prairie

5 what katy did

6 the wolves of willoughby chase

7 on the way home

8 dinosaurs and all that rubbish

GRAMMAR

Adverbs

> **Adverbs** are sometimes used in pairs to make meaning clearer, such as when we are comparing things or people.
>
> Our teacher climbed the Eiffel Tower **slowly**.
> *adverb*
>
> He climbed **more slowly** than me.
> *adverb adverb*
>
> These adverbs can also tell us more about other adverbs.
>
> quite   only   so   almost
> very   rather   less   most

A Write the adverbs in each of these sentences. The first is done to help you.

1 The teacher told us to walk less quickly.
(Answer: *less quickly*)

2 He said we should make our notes very neatly.

3 When he was cross he spoke to us extremely fiercely.

4 When he was pleased he spoke to us fairly quietly.

B Choose four different adverbs from the box on page 17 to improve the meaning of these sentences.

1 Paula fell down ____ heavily.

2 She bore the pain ____ bravely.

3 Our teacher said Paula was ____ slightly hurt.

4 She said she was ____ seriously hurt than she might have been.

Irregular verbs

> Some verbs are **regular**. This means the core of the word (its 'root') stays the same when the tense changes.
> *Example:* I **jump**, I **jumped** and I **have jumped**
>
> But many are **irregular** when the tense changes.
> *Example:* I **fly**, I **flew** and I **have flown**

A Copy the table and fill in the gaps.

Present tense	Simple past tense	Past tense with 'have', 'has' or 'had'
go	went	have gone
do	did	have done
sing	sang	have sung
eat	ate	have eaten
swim	swam	have swum
come	____	have come
break	broke	have ____
write	____	have written
bite	____	have ____
drink	____	have drunk
take	took	____ ____
speak	____	____ ____

SPELLING

Words from French

Look
Cover
Remember
Write
Check

> Here are some words which, because they have come from the French language, are not easy to spell or pronounce.
>
> campaign   memoirs   prestige   guardian   wage
> siege   fortress   marquis   viscount   banquet   mutton

A Choose eight of the words in the box to learn. Invent one sentence that includes at least four of these words.

B Find these words in your dictionary and write out their definitions.

prestige   memoirs   banquet   campaign   mutton

QUIZ

Towns and cities

Use your atlas to find the names of these towns and cities. Make a list in your book.

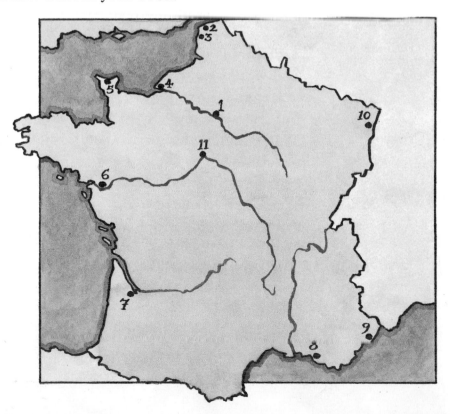

The flight of Icarus

An ancient Greek myth or legend tells the story of Daedalus, a great engineer and inventor. Daedalus and Icarus, his son, were being kept captive by the king of Crete on his island.

The king gave Daedalus a well-equipped workshop in a high tower, but even this was not enough to make the inventor content to remain in Crete. He just wanted his freedom to leave the island and return to his own country. Realising this, the king ordered that all the ships should be searched before leaving port to check that Daedalus and Icarus were not aboard. But the two were determined to leave, and if they could not escape by sea they would find another way!

Daedalus watched the birds and suddenly an idea came to him. That was it! He would build Icarus and himself a set of wings each.

He sent Icarus off to collect all the feathers he could find and soon the workshop was full of thousands of them. Next, Daedalus made a wooden frame shaped like the wing of a bird. He poured melted wax onto the frame, and into the wax he pressed the feathers. Then he let the wax cool and become solid again. To his delight, when he attached the wings to his shoulders, he could feel the wind trying to lift him into the air. Immediately he set to work to make a second pair for Icarus. Daedalus was sure that he and his son could jump from the tower and fly across the water.

When they were ready to leave Daedalus gave the boy some advice. "If you fly too low, the spray from the waves will make your wings wet and heavy, but if you fly too high, the heat from the sun will melt the wax that holds the feathers together. Stay near me and you will be safe."

With a feeling of great excitement they climbed onto the window ledge. Daedalus smiled at his son, then jumped. At first the wings did not seem to be lifting him. Desperately he flapped his wings and then, slowly at first, he was carried up into the sky. He glanced over his shoulder to see Icarus close behind.

What a thrill young Icarus felt, to be flying like a bird. With sheer delight, Icarus soared higher and higher up towards the clouds. Daedulus suddenly realised that his son was too excited to remember his father's warning. Up, up, soared the boy, through the clouds – and then above them.

"Icarus, my son! Come back, the sun will melt the wax!" pleaded Daedalus, but Icarus was now too far away to hear the cries of his father. Suddenly Icarus remembered. It was too late! He could see the feathers beginning to come away from the wooden frame – first a few, then more and more. He began to lose height. Faster and faster he fell towards the sea, with the feathers scattering around him as he crashed down past his desperate, helpless father.

Daedalus pulled the boy's still body from the sea and flew back to land where, weeping bitterly, he buried him.

Some time later Daedalus built a temple to Apollo, the god of sunlight. In it he hung his wings as an offering to the god. Never again would Daedalus fly.

COMPREHENSION

A Copy these sentences, filling in the missing words.

1 Daedalus was a great ____ and ____ .

2 His son, ____ , helped him in his workshop.

3 Icarus became too ____ to remember his father's instruction not to fly too high.

4 Daedalus wept ____ as he buried his son's body.

B Write sentences to answer these questions.

1 Why did Daedalus want to escape from Crete?

2 How did he get the idea for his escape plan?

3 Which words does the writer use to describe how Daedalus felt as he watched Icarus falling to his death?

4 Imagine that you could fly like a bird for one day. Make a list of words that you might use to describe the sensations you might experience.

Remember, **homophones** are words that *sound the same*, but which are *spelt differently*.
Example: Icarus could **see** the **sea**.

Homonyms are words that *sound and are spelt the same*, but which have *different meanings*.
Example: Don't crash into that **rock**.
Don't **rock** the boat.

A Write sentences using each of these words to show as many different meanings as possible. Use a dictionary to help you find the different definitions.

1 bank   2 club   3 fine
4 watch   5 box   6 hatch

PUNCTUATION

Conversations

Inverted commas are sometimes called speech marks.

Here is part of a conversation that might have taken place between Icarus and his father.

"Icarus, I need you to find me some feathers," said Daedalus. "Why do you need feathers?" asked the boy.
"You ask too many questions," his father replied. "Just do as I ask."
"But where do I start to look?" enquired Icarus. "I can't go simply asking the birds to lend me their feathers, can I?" he added, irritably.

Notice that a new line is started each time a different person starts to speak.

A Copy this next part of the conversation, adding the inverted commas and other missing punctuation marks, and starting a new line each time a different person starts to speak.

If you were clever you would not ask such silly questions said Daedalus Look there is a butcher's shop across the street, does that give you a clue Yes it does replied the boy I will go and ask them for the feathers from the chickens they have plucked That is more like it said Daedalus Now be as quick as you can We don't have much time

B Make up three or four more sentences that they may have said to finish this conversation.

GRAMMAR

More irregular verbs

A Copy these sentences, correcting the verbs in *italics*.

1 Icarus *bringed* the feathers to his father.

2 He *throwed* the feathers on the floor.

3 His father *come* across to look at them.

4 The boy *standed* waiting for his reaction.

5 "You have *did* well," said his father.

6 "I have *broke* some of them though," replied Icarus.

7 "Don't worry, you have *took* a lot of trouble," said Daedalus reassuringly.

8 Icarus should have *knew* that his father would be pleased.

SPELLING

Silent letters

Look
Cover
Remember
Write
Check

Many words have silent letters. Here are some to learn.

knee	wrestle	science	guard
knuckle	wriggle	scent	guide
knowledge	wrinkles	scenery	disguise

A Copy the list of words. Draw a neat circle round the silent letter or letters in each of them.

B Write four interesting sentences, each using a word from the bottom row in the box.

QUIZ

Greek tiles

How many three-, four- and five-letter words can you make from these tiles?

You are not allowed to use any tile more than once in any word.

23

The modern Olympics

The ancient Olympic Games were established about 3000 years ago as part of a religious festival to salute and honour the Greek gods, in particular Zeus. The festival contained many different competitions, including music and theatre performances, as well as sporting events.

In contrast, the modern Olympics are organised as a method of saluting the athletic talents of individual sportsmen and sportswomen from all nations, and for two weeks it is hoped that the conflict between different countries will be replaced by friendly competition.

The Olympic Games were completely forgotten for more than fifteen centuries, and during this time an earthquake and landslide destroyed and buried the original stadium.

In 1875 German archaeologists discovered pieces of the old stadium building, which gave a Frenchman, Pierre de Coubertin, an idea. He thought different nations would learn to live together more peacefully if their young men and women came together to compete and enjoy sports, so he organised an international sports congress, which launched the Olympic Games as we know them today. In honour of the ancient Olympics the first of the modern Olympic Games was held in Greece, at Athens in 1896, when thirteen countries competed in 42 events in nine different sports.

The nine sports in the first modern Olympics were:

cycling	tennis	athletics
fencing	shooting	weightlifting
gymnastics	swimming	wrestling

In 1924 the Winter Olympics were started and they, like the summer event and the original Greek festival, are held every four years.

Each time the Games are held they get bigger and more lavish, and they now generate vast amounts of money from sponsors and television companies, who are prepared to pay large sums to be involved.

COMPREHENSION

A Copy these sentences, putting a suitable word or words in the gap.

1 The first ancient Olympics were held around ____ years ago, and the modern Games were started in ____ .

2 There were more than ____ centuries between the last of the ancient Olympics and the first modern Olympics.

3 The 1896 Games had ____ different types of event.

4 As with the Summer Olympics, the Winter Games are held every ____ years.

B Write sentences to answer these questions.

1 Why were the original Games held?

2 What is one of the main differences between the ancient Olympic Games and those held now?

3 Why do you think that Pierre de Coubertin imagined that running the Games would help people to live together more peacefully? Do you think he was right?

4 If the ancient Greeks could see the modern Games, of what would they approve and of what would they disapprove?

Many English words have come from other languages.
Example: **athlon** is Greek. It means **contest**.
deci is Latin and means **tenth** or **ten**.

A Copy this chart, and fill in the missing numbers. You may need to use your dictionary. The first is done to help you.

		Clue
<u>dec</u>athlon	10	sports events
triathlon	____	sports events
pentathlon	____	sports events
pentagon	____	sides and angles
octagon	____	sides and angles
hexagon	____	sides and angles
bicycle	____	wheels
tricycle	____	wheels
biennial	____	years
century	____	years

Definitions

A Find these words in the text on pages 24 and 25, and use a dictionary or thesaurus to help you write another word which is a **synonym** and could be used instead of the word in the passage. The first is done to help you.

1 established = started   2 honour

3 conflict   4 original

5 lavish   6 generate

7 vast   8 sponsors

> **Prepositions**
> often tell us
> about *position*.

A **preposition** is a word that shows the relationship of a noun or a pronoun to another word in the sentence.
Example: The games were held **in** the stadium.

A Copy these **prepositions**, and next to each write its **antonym** (opposite) from the box. The first is done to help you.

1 inside / *outside*
2 below
3 off
4 before
5 up
6 near

above
outside
far
down
after
on

B Write out the prepositions in these sentences.

1 We went to the Games.
2 Three athletes jumped over the bar.
3 They ran around the track four times.
4 He received a medal from the judges.
5 The canoeists raced under the bridge.
6 The marathon runner fell on the uneven road.
7 As she ran into the arena the crowd went wild.
8 He ran the 100 metres sprint in less than ten seconds.
9 This prize is for you.
10 It was a close race between Sundip and Mark.

C The prepositions in bold are not correct. Write the sentences correctly.

1 She is quicker **from** me in the hurdles.
2 He climbed **of** the pedestal after receiving the gold medal.
3 Claire may not be **to** training today.
4 She dived gracefully **in** the water.
5 The crowd was full **off** excitement as she prepared for her last jump.

Using 'is/are' and 'was/were'

We usually use **is** and **was** if we are speaking or writing about one person or thing.
Example: Here **is** the medal I won.

We usually use **are** and **were** if we are speaking or writing about more than one person or thing.
Example: Here **are** the medals I won.

If we are writing about *you* (singular or plural) we always use **are** and **were**.
Example: You **are** a good runner.

A Write the word which you would use to complete these sentences.

1 There (is/are) a race starting soon.

2 There (was/were) three races earlier today.

3 Here (is/are) the winner's certificate.

4 (Is/Are) these children old enough to enter?

5 (Was/Were) you in the final this year?

6 There (was/were) a large plate of sandwiches for us to share.

7 Sara and Ben (wasn't/weren't) interested in athletics.

8 Kelly (isn't/aren't) able to run because of a strained muscle.

9 One of the sisters (was/were) always favourite to win.

10 Rick, James and Matt (was/were) in the relay team.

leisure	measure	treasure
exposure	pleasure	enclosure
disclosure	composure	displeasure

A From the box, select the correct word to complete the sentences. Use your dictionary if you need help.

1 I maintained my ____ despite all the noise around me.

2 The discovery of the ____ brought the archaeologist great ____ .

3 The Greeks enjoyed their sport and ____ time.

4 We now know that it is unwise to have too much ____ to the sun.

B Check the definition of each of these words in a dictionary. Then write an interesting sentence for each one to show that you know what it means.

1 displeasure 2 disclosure 3 measure 4 enclosure

Be careful – one will need a capital letter.

Anagrams are made by rearranging the letters of a word or phrase to make a new word or phrase. Can you solve these anagrams by rearranging the letters to make a word that fits the definition?

1 wrote – tall part of a castle

2 more – ancient city

3 ports – physical activity

4 earn – antonym of 'far'

Now make up some anagrams to challenge your friends.

Check-up 1

VOCABULARY

A Copy these sentences, filling each gap with either **should** or **would**.

1 Our teacher asked if we ____ like to have a disco.

2 I told him that I ____ like to come.

3 My friends said that they ____ like to come too.

B Write two sentences about the school disco for each of these homonyms, showing how words that are spelt the same can have more than one meaning.

1 watch   2 record   3 light

PUNCTUATION

A Add the capital letters and correct punctuation to each of these sentences.

1 wesley and paula are brilliant dancers

2 do you like this band

3 they're rubbish

4 i think they are quite good

B Write these titles, adding capital letters where necessary.

1 the encyclopedia of pop music

2 cliff turner and the rolling beetles

3 the flight of the bumble bee

4 how to play the guitar in ten easy lessons

C These sentences are part of a short conversation. Add the missing punctuation. Begin a new line where necessary.

Will your Mum let me walk home with her and you? asked Jo. Yes, of course, replied Marie, but we will have to leave just before the end. That's all right, said Jo, who had had enough dancing for one evening.

GRAMMAR

Some words can go in more than one list.

A Read this short paragraph.

All the class agreed that the disco last Monday was great fun. Crowds of people came, and the hall was really thumping away! Even though the music was very loud, none of the neighbours complained, except Mr Glum, but he always complains about noise.

Make lists of:

1 the common nouns

2 the proper nouns

3 the abstract nouns

4 the collective nouns

B Copy these sentences, but write a pronoun in place of each of the words or groups of words underlined.

1 Annie said I could wear <u>Annie's</u> top.

2 Dinesh and Russell asked if <u>Dinesh and Russell</u> could dance with us.

3 Afterwards Wesley said that <u>Wesley</u> had really enjoyed himself.

4 Mr Smith asked if we had liked <u>Mr Smith's</u> idea of having an end-of-term disco.

SPELLING

A Write the plural form of these words.

1 light   2 flash   3 box

4 try   5 watch   6 chair

B The same letter is missing from all of these words. Copy the words, filling in the missing letter or letters.

1 unti __   2 umbre __ a   3 grow __

4 wou __ d   5 beautifu __   6 fo __ ow

Life cycle of the common frog

Frogs spend the winter hibernating in muddy depressions or buried in damp, dark holes. They re-awaken to continue their complicated life cycle, which starts with the fertilisation of the eggs.

First the male, who is usually smaller than the female, returns to the pond and croaks loudly to attract her. As the female lays her eggs, the male releases his sperm to fertilise them. As the eggs swell with water they float to the surface as frogspawn. There can be up to 3000 eggs in a clump.

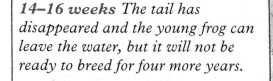

14–16 weeks *The tail has disappeared and the young frog can leave the water, but it will not be ready to breed for four more years.*

Day 1 *(after hatching) The tadpole attaches itself to a weed and feeds on the remaining food from the egg.*

Day 3 *Begins to take in oxygen through its external gills and to feed on tiny pieces of plant material.*

12 weeks *Front legs have formed and the eyes and mouth have become larger.*

8–10 weeks *Back legs have formed and air is breathed into the lungs, at the surface of the pond or creek.*

3 weeks *The external gills have shrunk and internal ones have grown.*

As the colder winter weather replaces the milder summer days and the frog's food supply (insects and worms) diminishes, it finds a shelter and hibernates until the following spring. Unfortunately, the sleepy frogs, as they first emerge from hibernation, often fall prey to other creatures looking for food, such as hedgehogs and herons.

Those frogs which survive the winter and are not eaten by other creatures, or killed by passing cars, arrive back at their ponds or creeks ready to recommence the life cycle.

Frog Fact File

- Frogs are amphibians – animals which can live on land but lay their eggs in water.
- Many frogs lay their eggs in clumps; others lay theirs in long strings.
- There are over 2500 species of frogs and toads.
- A common frog can jump 50 cm.
- The biggest frog is the African Goliath frog. It can have a body length of 30 cm.
- Frogs are *ectothermic*, which means their body temperature is always similar to their surroundings.
- The tadpole's body gradually changes into that of a small frog in about 16 weeks. This process is called *metamorphosis*.

Poison Arrow Frog from Costa Rica

A Copy these sentences, filling in the gaps.

1 The male frog is usually ____ than the female.

2 The female lays up to ____ eggs in a clump.

3 Frogs are ____ when they first wake from hibernation.

4 They may then become the ____ of other creatures.

B Write sentences to answer these questions.

1 How far can a common frog jump?

2 What does 'ectothermic' mean?

3 Make a list of the pleasures and another list of the problems of being a frog.

Girl collecting frogspawn

VOCABULARY

Using 'may' and 'can'

> **May** requests *permission* to do something.
> *Example:* **May** we go pond-dipping this afternoon?
>
> **Can** expresses the *ability* to do something.
> *Example:* I **can** see a large clump of frogspawn.

A Write these sentences, putting **may** or **can** in the gaps.

1 ____ we come with you?

2 ____ you see the frogs in the muddy water?

3 They ____ adjust their body temperature to match their surroundings.

4 ____ we take some frogspawn back to school?

5 You ____ if you ____ find a container, and if you promise to return the tadpoles to the pond later.

More prefixes

Remember, a prefix is a group of letters put at the front of a word.

Re is a **prefix** that can mean *again* or *back*.
Example: **re**arrange means arrange *again*

Ex is a **prefix** that can mean *out of* or *from*.
Example: **ex**port means to send goods *from* a country

A Find these **ex** and **re** words in the passage about frogs, then complete the definitions. Use a dictionary to check your answers.

1 External means _____ .

2 Return means _____ .

3 Release means _____ .

4 Replace means _____ .

5 Recommence means _____ .

B Select a word from the box to complete these sentences.

expected	relieved	extend	refused
exhausted	replace	express	recall

1 The teacher asked if we could ____ where we had found frogspawn last year.

2 He ____ that we would find some frogspawn in the same pond this year.

3 We enjoyed pond-dipping so much he allowed us to ____ our stay by an hour.

4 Our teacher ____ to touch any rare creatures or plants.

5 By the time we reached school we were all ____ after such a long walk.

C Write three interesting sentences which include the words

relieve   **express**   **replace**.

GRAMMAR

Adjectives and adverbs

Adverbs add to what we know about verbs!

Remember, **adjectives** give more information about nouns.

Examples: **green** frog   **muddy** pond   **last** year
         adjective noun   *adjective noun* *adjective noun*

Adverbs give us more information about verbs. They tell us how, when or where something happens.

Examples: hopped **quickly**   go **now**   come **here**
       verb   *adverb*   *verb adverb*   *verb adverb*

A Copy these sentences, and use a ruler to underline the adjectives in red and the adverbs in blue.

1 A little boy looked excitedly into a jar of frogspawn.

2 Walk quietly so as not to frighten the tiny creatures.

3 Tomorrow we shall go to the bigger pond.

4 We shall go there in the white minibus.

5 Gently she lifted the delicate creature on to her hand.

Phrases

Sometimes a single adjective or adverb is not enough to describe a particular noun or verb. Then we need to use two or three words. These groups of words are called **phrases**.

Examples: The frog, **cold and wet**, sat on her hand.
           The frog jumped **into the water**.

The first example describes **the frog** (a noun), so it is an **adjective phrase**.
The second example describes **jumped** (a verb), so it is an **adverb phrase**.

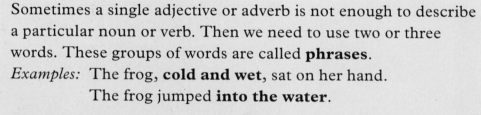

A Copy these sentences. Underline a phrase in each and write *adjective phrase* or *adverb phrase* after it. The first is done to help you.

1 They were sitting on the bank of the river.
    They were sitting <u>on the bank of the river</u>. *adverb phrase*

2 We ran as fast as our legs would carry us.

3 The male frog, smaller than the female, was croaking loudly.

4 The newts, sleek and delicate, could be seen basking in the sun.

5 We sat quietly and attentively, watching the female frog.

6 Her tiny but energetic tadpoles were eating the weeds.

Look
Cover
Remember
Write
Check

| discussion | impression | expression | procession |
| profession | depression | digression | permission |

A Copy this short paragraph, selecting one of the words from the box to fill each of the gaps.

The kind old lady next door gave us ____ to climb over her fence. She said that when she was younger her ____ was teaching, and we had a fascinating ____ with her about the wide variety of creatures which lived in the pond that had developed in the small, muddy ____ at the bottom of her garden.

M E T A M O R P H O S I S

QUIZ

High scorer

How many words can you make from the letters in this word?

Score
- **1** for each one-letter word
- **2** for each two-letter word
- **3** for each three-letter word
- **4** for each four-letter word
- **6** for each five-letter word
- **8** for each six-letter word
- **10** for each seven-letter word

Bonus! If you can find words with more than seven letters, score twice the number of letters in the word.

The moon

Of our Earth's many satellites only one is natural – the moon. It has puzzled, frightened or fascinated people on Earth for thousands of years. Some have worshipped it and others were sure there were strange creatures living there. The moon is very important to us. At night it reflects light from the sun – nights are much less dark when there is a full moon shining brightly. It is also the pull from the gravity of the moon that causes our tides to ebb and flow twice each day.

We know that the moon was formed at about the same time as the Earth, about $4\frac{1}{2}$ thousand million (4,500,000,000) years ago, which may mean that it was formed as a separate body in the solar system and was later 'captured' by the Earth's gravity. There are, however, other theories for its origin. Some scientists used to believe it was a huge part of the Earth which broke away, leaving the enormous depression in the surface of the Earth which is now filled by the Pacific Ocean.

The diameter of the moon is about a quarter of that of the Earth, which means that if it could be placed on the surface of the Earth it would approximately fit on top of Australia.

The moon is almost a quarter of a million miles (384,000 kilometres) away, and orbits the Earth once every $27\frac{1}{3}$ days. The moon also 'rotates' once in roughly the same time. Therefore, from Earth we see only one side of the moon, although cameras have sent back pictures of the hidden 'dark' side.

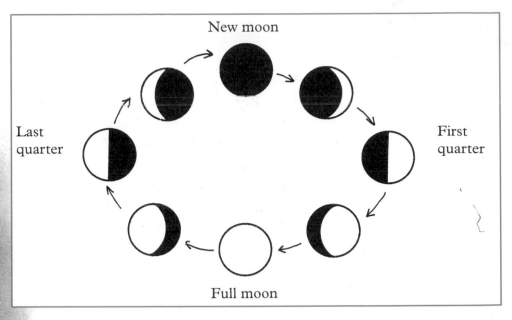

New moon

Last
quarter

First
quarter

Full moon

The phases of the moon

As the moon orbits the Earth, different portions are lit by the sun. The changing appearance this produces is known as the moon's phases. Every month it goes from the 'new' moon phase, which looks like a C backwards, to the 'full' moon phase, when we see a full circle, and then to the 'old' moon which looks like a normal C, and on to the new moon again.

The moon, like Earth, does not have any light of its own. The light we see on the moon is reflected from the sun. About twice a year the Earth passes between the moon and the sun and this causes a shadow of the Earth to fall on the moon. This is called an eclipse of the moon.

A Copy these sentences, filling in the gaps.

1 The moon is about the same age as the _____ .

2 It is the only natural _____ of the Earth.

3 The diameter of the moon and the width of _____ are similar.

4 'New moon' and 'full moon' are _____ of the moon.

B Write sentences to answer these questions.

1 How much larger is the diameter of the Earth than that of the moon?

2 Approximately how many times does the moon orbit the Earth in one year?

3 How do we know what is on the hidden side of the moon?

4 Write in your own words what causes an eclipse of the moon.

VOCABULARY

Idioms

Idioms are short phrases which mean something quite differen
from what might be expected.
Example: To be **over the moon** about something
means to be delighted about it.

Ali was **over the moon** about passing his exam.

A Match each of the **idioms** with its correct meaning – copy them
out and draw lines to connect them. Draw a humorous cartoon to
illustrate the literal meaning of one of the idioms.

1	over the moon	a gloomy person
2	bark up the wrong tree	get into trouble
3	a wet blanket	wise for his or her age
4	bring the house down	delighted ✓
5	get into hot water	have the wrong idea ✓
6	an old head on young shoulders	cause great amusement ✓

B Finish these idioms and say what they mean.

1 To hit the nail on the ____ .

2 To put all your cards on the ____ .

3 To live from hand to ____ .

4 To blow your own ____ .

5 To see things through rose-coloured ____ .

GRAMMAR

Verbs
Active and passive

Remember, the
subject is the main
thing or person
related to the verb.

Verbs are **active** when the subject of the sentence *does* the action.
Example: The **astronaut flew** the shuttle.
     subject   *active verb*

Verbs are **passive** when the subject of the sentence has the
action *done to it*.
Example: The **shuttle was flown** by the astronaut.
     subject *passive verb*

A Rewrite these sentences with the verb changed from active to
passive, so that the subject has the action done to it.
The first is done to help you.

1 An asteroid hit the space vehicle.
The space vehicle was hit by an asteroid.

2 The moon orbits the Earth.

40

3 Craters cover the moon.

4 The scientists watched the eclipse of the moon.

5 A spacesuit protects the astronaut.

6 The captain landed the Shuttle.

B Now write these sentences with the verbs changed from passive to active.

1 The moon was hit by a small meteorite.

2 The spacecraft was knocked off course by a faulty jet.

3 The Earth's oceans are affected by the moon's pull.

4 Some children are frightened by the 'Man in the Moon' story.

SPELLING

Double consonants

Look
Cover
Remember
Write
Check

Each of these words has a double consonant missing.
Copy the list, adding the missing consonants.

1 spe ____ ing   2 su ____ ose   3 di ____ er

4 su ____ enly   5 e ____ ect   6 co ____ ence

7 spa ____ er   8 e ____ ort   9 co ____ ect

10 co ____ and   11 sho ____ ing   12 wi ____ er

QUIZ

Hidden words

There are sixteen words about space hidden in this puzzle. They go down or across. Time how long it takes you to find all the words.

a	x	o	r	b	i	t	g	c	e
s	d	g	a	l	a	x	y	o	c
t	M	u	s	u	n	w	k	m	l
e	a	s	t	a	r	s	m	e	i
r	r	y	r	o	c	k	e	t	p
o	s	w	o	e	n	y	d	s	s
i	t	a	n	l	m	o	o	n	e
d	p	l	a	n	e	t	s	x	z
V	e	n	u	s	o	n	o	v	a
q	z	p	t	m	e	t	e	o	r

41

Cosmic poem

This poem, in which the poet sets out to give us two messages, was written some years ago.

It's very well that we shall soon
Be landing chaps upon the Moon
(She who we poets specially honour)
And planting little flags upon her;
And that the next stop will be Venus;
And we'll be sharing out between us
The planets and the planetoids
Rambling through azoic voids.

Before we start it might be fit
We tidied up this Earth a bit.
We've got a very ugly bomb
Can blow us all to Kingdom Come
Unless we mind our Ps and Qs;
And it will be no earthly use
Cavorting round the galaxies
If, down here, radio-active seas
Upon an uninhabited shore
Roll sadly on for evermore.
What life may be among the stars
Or basks along the canals of Mars –
The bug-eyed monsters and puce rabbits –
I hope will not adopt our habits.

Another fact worth pointing out
In the context of this kick-about
(I know of course it's obvious,
And do not wish to make a fuss;
But still I think we really ought
To give the matter serious thought
To save us from undue elation
And cosmic self-congratulation) –
Is this: well more than half the mortals
Who pass beyond the womb's dark portals
And blindly struggle into birth
Here, on this unromantic Earth,
To grow up under mundane skies,

Go hungry to bed, and hungry rise –
And are neither healthy, wealthy nor wise.

Outer Space can wait its turn:
The human being's my concern.

John Heath-Stubbs

COMPREHENSION

A Copy these sentences, filling in the gaps.

1 The poet suggests that after astronauts have landed on the moon, they will next be heading for ____ .

2 He is worried that we have a 'very ugly ____ '.

3 He is also concerned about people who go to bed ____ .

4 The poet says his main concern is for ____ ____ ____ .

B Write sentences to answer these questions.

1 How do you know that *Cosmic Poem* was written some years ago?

2 What are the poet's two main concerns?

3 What do you think the poet means by:

   azoic voids
   cavorting
   mundane?

4 Do you think John Heath-Stubbs approves of space exploration? Give some reasons for your answer.

VOCABULARY

Contractions

'Contract' means 'make smaller'.

Remember, **contractions** are two words run together as one. We often do this when we speak. When we write we use an apostrophe (') to show that letters are missing.
Examples: **we'll** be sharing out (*we will*)
of course **it's** obvious (*it is*)

A Write these contractions out in full.

1	it's	2	what's	3	they'll
4	I'll	5	he'll	6	who'd
7	wouldn't	8	haven't	9	can't

B What contractions might be used for the words in italics?

1 *You will* not be able to see the eclipse from here.

2 *It is* about 240,000 miles from Earth to the moon.

3 "If we land *we will* never take off again," shouted the astronaut.

4 You *must not* look directly at the sun.

5 She *has not* used a telescope before.

GRAMMAR

Double negatives

Think about what this sentence really means!

No, **not**, **nothing**, **never**, **nowhere** and contractions with **n't** are called **negative words**.
Examples: I have a telescope. *positive*
I do **not** have a telescope. *negative*
If we were to put *two* **negative** words in one sentence, they would cancel each other out. They would *reverse* the meaning of the sentence.
Example: I do **not** have **no** telescope.

A Write these sentences in your book. Neatly underline the negative words, and then write each sentence with the meaning the writer probably intended. The first is done to help you.

1 I <u>haven't</u> got <u>no</u> money to buy a telescope.
I haven't any money to buy a telescope.

2 We looked carefully but we couldn't see no moon.

3 They can never see nothing.

4 He will never try nothing new.

5 The boys weren't going nowhere special tonight.

6 Wesley will get cold as he hasn't got no gloves on.

7 Mum said she could not get no hot chocolate today.

8 "We never did nothing wrong," they claimed.

9 "You're never no help when I need you," said Mum.

10 "We couldn't see nothing with that telescope," said James.

SPELLING

Silent 'h'

Look
Cover
Remember
Write
Check

ch usually makes the sound as in **ch**ess and mu**ch**, but sometimes the **h** is a silent letter.

Read the words in the box.

headache	echo	choir	chemist	stomach
school	architect	Christmas	orchestra	chorus

A Choose a word from the box to fill the gaps in this short paragraph.

Andrew was always very interested at ____ when they were learning about space. His mother therefore knew his ____ must be bad if he wanted to stay at home, especially as the ____ was practising today for the ____ concert, and he wanted to be in it. She said she would go to the ____ and buy some tablets, which would make him feel better very soon.

QUIZ

No space!

This is one sentence. All the capital letters and punctuation have been omitted, as have the spaces between the words. Write it out properly.

ibelievesaidjohnheathstubbsthatspaceexplorationislessimportantthan caringforpeopleonearth

Family at war

War causes terrible suffering and great sadness. During the Second World War, families everywhere were split up; fathers, uncles and brothers spent many years away in the army, navy or air force, or helped in the ambulance services. Many women joined the women's services or moved away to work in the factories and on farms, doing the jobs left by the servicemen. Also, many mothers worked long hours in voluntary services or in factories while their children were at school, keeping the country supplied with all the goods that were needed.

Eileen Frost was a young woman living in Portsmouth when the war started. After the war she wrote about her memories of 1939.

'I listened to the radio broadcast by Chamberlain, our Prime Minister, in our sitting room. He said that the British government had asked Adolf Hitler to promise not to invade Poland, but I will always remember when he said, "No such assurance has been received, and therefore from this time, we are at war with Germany." I remember a dreadful feeling of apprehension such as my mother must have felt at the onset of World War I.

'Changes came immediately. First of all a total blackout was ordered. Black cotton curtains had to be made for all the windows, and afterwards, when these were found not to be sufficiently effective, black paint and black paper were used around the edges. Not a glimmer of light was permitted to be seen. It caused some amusement when our vicar's wife put a light on and crossed the room to pull the curtains. She should, of course, have pulled the curtains first. A warden knocked on her door and she was taken to court and fined for breaking the law, and she the vicar's wife!

'Torches were allowed, to enable people to find their way in pitch darkness in the unlit streets, but these had to have only a small spot of light. I remember once, out alone after dark, getting completely lost in an area with which I was entirely familiar, and having

War is declared

DATE

The imminence of war came as a complete shock to us and to many people.

— "no such assurance has been received, and therefore, from this time, we are at war with Germany"

Sept. 3rd 1939

NATIONAL
REGISTRATION

IDENTITY
CARD

to search to find a road name with my tiny torch before I could find my way home.

'We all helped to dig a hole in the back garden for the Anderson air-raid shelter which had been issued. It was made of corrugated steel about 6 feet (2 metres) by 8 feet (about 2½ metres) and had to be sunk 4 feet (over 1 metre) into the ground. Its rounded roof had then to be covered with earth to provide extra protection, and a wooden door and steps made for its entrance at one end. We even made a flowerbed on top!

'We were all issued with gas masks in anticipation that the enemy would use poison gas as in the Great War. We stretched them over our heads – and they gave us a sort of pig-like snouted appearance. We could just see out of a small transparent frame. As it happened, gas wasn't used in World War II.

'At first the shops were well stocked, but gradually we became aware that various things were not available. Some imported fruits like bananas were not seen for over six years.

'Within a few months there were great changes for us. The first bombs fell on Portsmouth and we had our first sight of bomb damage, part of our school in Drayton Road, North End, was demolished, and the dockyard and a pub called the Air Balloon were also damaged.

'When the sirens sounded we would hurry into our shelter. Sometimes we could hear the crump of dropping bombs and the thunderous gunfire as we tried to talk together. Inwardly all of us were quaking with fear and hoping and praying that the next bomb would not be for us. After four or five sleepless hours the "All Clear" would sound and we would gather up our belongings and blankets, cushions, flasks for hot drinks etc, and make our weary way out into the rain or cold, back to our beds at 4 or 5 o'clock in the morning to try to grab a few hours' sleep before the next day.'

COMPREHENSION

A Copy these sentences, using one or more words to fill the gaps.

1 Eileen Frost lived in ____ .

2 She helped her family dig a ____ for ____ .

3 The gunfire made ____ .

4 War causes terrible ____ and great ____ .

B Write sentences to answer these questions.

1 What was 'the blackout'?

2 Why was Eileen 'quaking with fear' whilst in the shelter?

3 Which weapon, used in the Great War, was not used in the Second World War?

4 Think of the reasons why 'war causes terrible suffering and great sadness'.

VOCABULARY

'Among' and 'between'

We share something **among** more than two people.
Example: We shared the hot drink **among** all four of us in the shelter.

We use **between** when we refer to two people only.
Example: Eileen and her mother shared the hot drink **between** them.

We also use **between** when there is no question of sharing.
Example: Mum let me choose **between** parsnips, turnips and cabbage for lunch.

Drayton Road School, Portsmouth, after an air raid attack

A Complete these sentences, using **among** or **between**.

1 My sister and I shared ____ us the job of keeping the shelter clean.

2 Mum said I was to share the food scraps ____ all the chickens.

3 The limited food available was divided ____ all the hungry people as fairly as possible.

4 It was difficult choosing ____ reading, listening to the gramophone, talking or playing games to keep us cheerful.

5 Grandad would often give the two children a bag of conkers to share ____ them.

Hyphens

> Compound words are made by joining two smaller words together.
> *Examples:* dock + yard = dockyard
> flower + bed = flowerbed
>
> If we want to join words to make **compound adjectives**, the words are often joined with a **hyphen** (-).
> *Examples:* air-raid shelter
> kind-hearted gentleman

A Write a **compound adjective** for each of the following. One part of the compound word is given. Find the second part in the box.

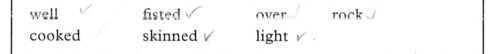

well ✓	fisted ✓	over ✓	rock ✓
cooked	skinned ✓	light ✓	

1 A person who speaks well. ____ -spoken

2 Someone likely to steal. ____ -fingered

3 Mean, and not likely to share. tight- ____

4 A person who is not easily offended. thick- ____

5 Something which is said to be better than it is. ____ -rated

6 Meat taken from the oven too soon. under- ____

7 Bread that has gone very stale. ____ -hard

B Use compound adjectives to express the following phrases more concisely. The first is done to help you.

1 An animal with keen eyes.
A keen-eyed animal.

2 A girl with curly hair.

3 A boy with long hair.

4 A man who works hard.

5 A horse with a strong will.

6 A liquid with an evil smell.

PUNCTUATION

Divided direct speech

Remember, direct speech is when we write the exact words a person has spoken.

Words such as **Eileen said**, **warned Norman** or **I said** may come before, in the middle of, or at the end of the words that are spoken.

Example: "Mum," said the anxious child, "I hope there won't be any bombs tonight."

A Copy these sentences, adding the missing punctuation marks.

1 Draw the curtains said Dad or the warden will soon be knocking at our door

2 Get in the shelter now insisted Joan urgently if you don't want to be killed

3 I have some potatoes said the frustrated shopkeeper but there'll be no fruit this week

4 Be patient advised Dad it is better to be safe than sorry

GRAMMAR

Using 'did' and 'done'

Remember, auxiliary (helping) verbs are words such as **had**, **have**, and **has**.

We *always* use an auxiliary (helping) verb when we write **done**.
Example: She **had done** her best.
      auxiliary verb
We *never* use an auxiliary verb with **did**.
Example: She **did** her best.

A Write these sentences, using the correct verb.

1 Show them how you (did/done) it.

2 We have (did/done) this before.

3 Please show me what you have (did/done).

4 Who (did/done) most of the work?

5 When they (did/done) the last part it cracked.

6 Now they have (did/done) it again it looks fine.

7 I (did/done) my best to help.

SPELLING

'ance' or 'ence' endings?

Look
Cover
Remember
Write
Check

entrance	ambulance	insurance	nuisance
experience	patience	audience	silence

A Copy and complete these sentences using words from the box.

1 The ____ crew had many years' ____ .

2 They worked slowly and with great ____ .

3 The police blocked off the ____ to our road, which was a ____ ,
but no one complained.

4 Very soon there was a large ____ , watching in ____ , as the
injured were lifted from the rubble.

B Write a definition from a dictionary for each of these words.

1 convenience   2 assistance   3 ignorance

4 remembrance   5 conscience   6 innocence

QUIZ

What's missing?

These are the middle four letters of nine six-letter words, all of
which begin with the same letter. Write down the words you can
work out.

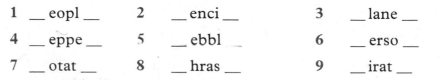

1 __ eopl __   2 __ enci __   3 __ lane __

4 __ eppe __   5 __ ebbl __   6 __ erso __

7 __ otat __   8 __ hras __   9 __ irat __

Check-up 2

A Copy these sentences, filling each gap with one of the words in the brackets.

1 "____ we come to watch you in the school sports?" asked his mother. (May/Can)

2 "____ you get the time off work then?" replied Andrew. (May/Can)

3 "My boss said I ____ leave an hour or two early if we're not too busy," said Mum. (may/can)

4 "Will you bring some sweets that I can share ____ all my friends? " he asked. (among/between)

5 "I don't know about that," said Mum, "but I'll have enough to share ____ you and Ali." (among/between)

B Write what Mum meant by these idioms.

1 "Don't <u>blow your own trumpet</u> if you win."

2 "I thought your friends would <u>bring the house down</u> when you went up to collect your prize."

3 "Dad would have been <u>over the moon</u> to see you today."

C Write the contraction for each of these pairs of words.

1	is not	2	I will
3	have not	4	who would
5	they will	6	we shall
7	can not	8	it is

Write these sentences as a conversation, adding the missing capital letters and punctuation marks, and beginning new lines where necessary.

i thought our team would win said andrew so did i replied fiona until i realised robert was in their team he is the fastest runner ive ever seen said andrew with a sigh and its just my luck that he is running against me in the next race don't worry said fiona comforting her brother just do your best

GRAMMAR

A Copy these sentences, underlining one adjective and drawing a neat circle around one adverb in each.

1 All the other runners seemed taller, Andrew thought, as he lined up anxiously.

2 In his new trainers, Andrew ran faster than he had ever run.

3 Fiona and Mum shouted excitedly as he ran through the white finishing tape.

B What can you find wrong with these sentences? Write them correctly.

1 Andrew done well to win the race.

2 He's never did that well before.

3 Everyone in our team done their best.

4 You shouldn't not let yourself get cold after the race.

5 Mark said he couldn't see nothing from where he was.

SPELLING

A Copy these words, filling in the missing letters.

1 su __ __ enly   2 ho __ __ ow   3 su __ __ ess

4 entr __ nce   5 audi __ nce   6 nuis __ nce

B Write the words to match these definitions.

1 a group of singers

2 a person who designs buildings

3 the time when Santa Claus is busy

The Giant of Grabbist

Just behind Dunster, a village in Somerset, is a steep hill called Grabbist. The legend of the Giant of Grabbist has been written down just as an old village gentleman told it, and as he remembers it being told to him when he was a child.

Bristol Channel

MINEHEAD
EXMOOR • • DUNSTER
Somerset
Devon
Cornwall

'We haven't got many giants about in Somerset, but we have one down here at Dunster. Ah! Come up from Cornwall, he did, and he didn't like staying in Devon, 'cos his cousins there was a bit rough like. He come up to Exmoor, nice peaceful friendly place it is. But the folk on Exmoor they didn't like the size of him; bit scared they was. But then they found out he didn't harm anyone. They got quite fond of him. And then farmers' wives they began to put their heads together. "What does the poor great fellow feed on?"

'Well, I think they were ready to cook a dinner for him, but they found they needn't. You see, he was fond of fish. He did wade out down channel right out to sea, and all the fishing boats had to do was to follow him. Oh! they come into Minehead harbour loaded, they did. He'd go and wade out there, and water come up to his armpits, and he'd scoop up great shoals o' fish, and 'twas a wonderful time for the fishing boats.

'Well now, one time old Elijah Crowcombe in the leaky old *Dorcas Jane* was loaded right up and she was a-wallowing in the waves when a storm comes up. Well, they thought they was a-going down, when through the storm the giant comes a-striding, and he picks up *Dorcas Jane*, and afore they could say "thank you", he puts her down quiet and safe like in Watchet harbour.

54

'Well now, Giant he was very happy on Exmoor, and then the Old Nick came back 'cos he didn't like seeing the little thatched churches going up all over the way. So when the folk of Hawkridge thought they'd build themselves a church, and Giant would help them, Old Nicky didn't like it. Ah! So when Giant was coming by Spire Cross, with a load of great stones, Old Nicky tripped him, and stones went all abroad.

'Well, Giant didn't say nothing, he didn't lose his temper as Old Nicky hoped he would, and cause a storm. No, he just patiently bent, and he picked them up one after another, and he put them up on Hawkridge for the church. And a great broken one he tossed into the very wood where the Old Boy was sat chuckling, and that made him go off in a hurry. And the rest of the stones, that weren't no good for churches, he laid them across the river Barle, and made Tarr Steps.

'Well, Giant he made up his mind that there wasn't no room for him and Old Nicky up on the moor, and Old Nicky he just about made up his mind the same. So two o' them got together Porlock way, and they said they'd have a competition like. They'd each throw a big stone from Bossington Beacon over to Porlock Common, that be four miles, and whoever lost would have to leave the place for good and all.

'Well, Old Nick had first throw, and his stone it flew out over the four miles and it landed up on Porlock Common. And then Old Nick he trips up Giant, and his stone fell only three feet away. But Giant he didn't go away. No, he just trips Old Nick himself and sat right down on him, and just smoked a pipe quiet-like, while Old Nick squirmed underneath. When he finished his pipe he picks up Old Nick by his tail, and he said, "That weren't a fair throw. We'll throw from Quantock later on. Meantime, you go cool your head." And he tossed Old Nick right out down channel, out over Porlock Bay.

'Giant picked up his stone and throwed right over to Battlegore, six mile away! "Your turn now," he says. Old Nicky was dancing with rage, and I think he was so cross about it, that his stone fell down, and the giant's was the furthest off. "Now," says the giant, "'tis your promise to go away from here, and never come back no more. But as no one can trust you, I'll make sure." And he picked up Old Nicky by his tail, and he waded out down the Severn Channel, till he was right out to sea, 'twas up to his armpits. And then he gave him a good swing three times round his head, and let go. Well, I reckon the Old 'Un landed about the West Indies!'

COMPREHENSION

A Copy these sentences, filling in the missing words.

1 ＿＿＿ is the steep hill behind Dunster.

2 Giant's favourite food was ＿＿＿ .

3 At first people were frightened of the giant, then they realised he didn't ＿＿＿ anyone.

4 Old Nicky and the giant had a ＿＿＿ to see which of them would stay, and which would go.

B Write sentences to answer these questions.

1 What evidence did the villagers have that he was a kindly giant?

2 What did Giant do with the stones which were unsuitable for building Hawkridge church?

3 What other names did the storyteller use for Old Nicky?

4 Do you think this story is true? What is a legend? Use a dictionary to help you.

VOCABULARY

Proverbs

Proverbs are well-known, wise sayings. Many are centuries old, handed down from generation to generation.

Example: Don't count your chickens before they're hatched.

"Don't count your chickens before they're hatched!"

A Write a sentence to explain the meaning of each of these proverbs.

1 James: You were lucky. When I called at the shop they had sold out.

Sarah: Ah! **The early bird catches the worm**.

2 Ian: The man who sold me this watch said I was lucky to get it for half price – but it won't work, and he's vanished!

Rick: **A fool and his money are soon parted**.

3 Mark: If he breaks my calculator, I'll break his!

Fiona: **Two wrongs don't make a right**.

B Choose the correct ending for each of these proverbs, and say what each means.

1 Empty vessels   lie
2 More haste   shouldn't throw stones
3 A stitch in time   the mice will play
4 When the cat's away   less speed
5 People who live in glass houses   make the most noise
6 Birds of a feather   saves nine
7 Let sleeping dogs   flock together

When we speak, we often use words less precisely than when we write. This legend is written just as the old gentleman told it, in his colourful Somerset dialect. When we write for most purposes, we use English more accurately. This is called 'standard English'.

Remember, **was** is singular and **were** is plural.

Write these sentences choosing the words we would use in standard English.

A Use **was** or **were** in each gap.

1 His cousins ____ a bit rough like.

2 They didn't like the size of him; bit scared they ____ .

3 They thought they ____ a-going down.

4 That ____ n't a fair throw!

B Change the words underlined to those used when writing standard English.

1 They <u>come</u> into Minehead harbour, they did.

2 He'd go and wade out there, and water <u>come</u> up to his armpits.

3 She was a-wallowing in the waves when a storm <u>comes</u> up.

4 He <u>puts</u> her down <u>quiet</u> and <u>safe</u>.

5 A great broken one he tossed where the Old Boy was <u>sat</u> chuckling.

6 Giant picked up his stone and <u>throwed</u> it over to Battlegore.

7 Then he <u>gived</u> him a good swing three times round his head.

C Think of words that might have been used instead of **nice** and **got** in these sentences. You might need to write some of the sentences a slightly different way.

1 We haven't got many giants about in Somerset.

2 He come up to Exmoor, nice peaceful friendly place it is.

3 They got quite fond of him.

4 The two o' them got together Porlock way.

SPELLING

'gue' endings

A **monologue** is when one person speaks by himself or herself. The passage is a record of the old gentleman's **monologue**.

Monolog**ue** has a silent **u**.
All the words in the box have an ending with a silent **u**.

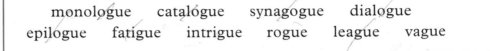

> monologue   catalogue   synagogue   dialogue
> epilogue   fatigue   intrigue   rogue   league   vague

A Write the answer for each of these definitions. Use the words from the box.

1 Book giving details of items listed

2 Extreme weariness

3 An organised collection of sports teams

4 A speech by one person

5 Scheming for bad reasons

6 Not clear

7 Jewish place of worship

8 Someone up to no good

9 A conversation

10 A passage at the end of a book

QUIZ

What do they mean?

People from certain areas or in certain jobs often use words or phrases that 'outsiders' find difficult to understand. Try to work out what these people are saying. Write down each person's speech and your 'translation'.

Make a list of phrases from your part of the country that outsiders might have difficulty in understanding.

A "This roo looks a bit crook to me, mate!"

B "Haud yer wheesht, you'll wake the weans!"

The Man Who Had No Story

There was to be a fair in Macroom on a certain day, and Rory O'Donoghue left home the evening before with his bag of stockings to sell them at the fair next day. Night came before he reached the town and he began to feel very weary, so when he saw a light in a cottage at the roadside, he knocked on the door. Inside was an old man with a long white beard.

The old man with the long white beard said he could stay and welcome. A chair that was at the bottom of the kitchen moved up toward the fire, and the old man told Rory to sit on it.

"Now," said the old man, "Rory O'Donoghue and myself would like to have our supper."

A knife and a fork jumped up from the dresser and cut pieces of meat from a knuckle joint that was hanging from the rafters. A pot came out of the dresser, and the meat hopped into it. A bucket of water rose up, and water was poured over the meat. Potatoes jumped into the bucket of water, and washed themselves. They then rose up and went into the pot. The knife and fork took the meat and potatoes from the pot and put them on a plate. A tablecloth spread itself on the table. The plate of food jumped onto the table and so did two knives, two forks and a pot of pickle. A knife and fork cut the meat into two portions and put some on each plate.

"Come, Rory O'Donoghue," said the old man. "Let us eat!"

"Whew, I'm full," sighed Rory contentedly as he finished.

"Loosen the buckles, and take off your shoes, Rory," said the old man. "Every evening I sit here telling stories. Tell a story for me now, Rory."

"I've never told a story in my life," replied Rory.

"Well, unless you tell a story, you'll have to leave," insisted the old man.

"But I can't tell stories," pleaded Rory.

"Off, out of the door with you then," said the old man firmly.

Rory stood up dejectedly, and collected his bag of stockings. He trudged off forlornly along the dark lane, but he hadn't gone far when he heard the crackle of burning logs and saw the glow of a fire by the roadside. By the fire was a man, roasting a piece of meat.

"You're welcome, Rory O'Donoghue," said the man. "Would you mind, Rory, taking hold of this spit and turning the meat over the fire? But don't let it burn!"

No sooner had Rory taken hold of the spit than the man left him. Then the piece of meat spoke.

"Don't let me burn," it shouted.

Rory threw the spit and the meat from him, snatched up his bag of stockings, and ran off as fast as he could. The spit and the piece of meat followed him, striking Rory O'Donoghue as hard as they could on the back.

"Ouch! Stop that," shouted Rory.

Soon Rory caught sight of the cottage of the old man with the long white beard.

"Welcome back, Rory O'Donoghue," said the old man. "Come in and rest for the night."

"Oh, I couldn't," said Rory. "I didn't tell you a story, and now I'm speckled with blood!"

"What happened?" asked the old man.

"Oh! The abuse I had from a piece of meat that a man was roasting," said Rory. "He asked me to turn the meat on the spit for a while, and 'twasn't long till the meat screamed at me not to burn it. I threw it from me, but it followed me, giving me heavy blows on the back, so that I'm all cut and bruised."

"Ah, Rory," chuckled the old man. "If only you had had a story like that to tell me, when I asked you. Lie in bed now, and sleep for the rest of the night."

Rory slipped into the soft, comfortable bed and fell sound asleep; but when he awoke in the morning, he found himself on the roadside, with his bag of stockings under his head, and not a trace of the cottage – or the old man with the long white beard.

A Copy these sentences, filling in the missing words.

1 Rory was heading for ____ to sell his stockings at the fair.

2 The old man had a long ____ ____ .

3 Rory didn't know any ____ to tell.

4 This made the old man cross, and he made Rory ____ the cottage.

B Write sentences to answer these questions.

1 Why did Rory stop on his way to the fair?

2 What meal did Rory share with the old man?

3 List some adjectives, and then use them in sentences, to describe how Rory must have felt when all the strange things began to happen around him. Your thesaurus might help you.

4 What do you think really happened to Rory that night?

VOCABULARY

Interjections

Hey! Don't use too many interjections in your writing!

An **interjection** is a word or group of words that expresses emotion.

If the interjection expresses a strong feeling it is used with an **exclamation mark**, and if it expresses mild emotion it is used with a **comma**.

Examples: "Whew, I'm full," sighed Rory.
"Ouch! That hurt!" exclaimed Rory.

Here are some commonly-used interjections.

Oh   Ah   Ouch   Oops   Hurrah   Help   Wow   Whew   Ugh

A Write sentences using these interjections with an exclamation mark.

1 Oh   2 Ouch   3 Help

B Write sentences using these interjections with a comma.

1 Help   2 Ah   3 Whew

We often use direct speech when writing stories, as it makes the characters appear more realistic. Look back at the story about Rory and the old man, and notice how a new line is used each time a different person starts to speak.

Example:

"Whew, I'm full," sighed Rory contentedly as he finished.

"Loosen the buckles, and take off your shoes, Rory," said the old man. "Every evening I sit here telling stories. Tell a story for me now, Rory."

"I've never told a story in my life," replied Rory.

"Well, unless you tell a story, you'll have to leave," insisted the old man.

"But I can't tell stories," pleaded Rory.

"Off, out of the door with you then," said the old man firmly.

A Write this paragraph, adding and correcting the punctuation marks, and starting new lines where necessary.

Wherever have you been Rory demanded his wife as soon as he returned from the fair, half anxious, half annoyed at his lateness. I have had a most incredible experience Rory tried to explain, still trembling each time he thought of the old man and his cottage. All I want to know is that you sold those stockings. I hope you sold them all husband she said threateningly. Yes I think so he responded still lost in a world he was struggling to understand. Whatever do you mean she snapped.

B Continue the conversation yourself, as Rory struggles to explain what happened on the way to the fair.

Remember, an **adjective phrase** is a small group of words that tells us more about a *noun* in a sentence, and an **adverb phrase** is a small group of words that tells us more about a *verb* in a sentence.

Examples: Inside was an old *man* <u>with a long white beard</u>.
(*adjective phrase about the 'man' – a noun*)

Rory *ran* <u>as fast as he could</u>.
(*adverb phrase about how he 'ran' – a verb*)

Phrases don't have a proper verb.

A Copy these sentences. Underline a phrase in each and write *adjective phrase* or *adverb phrase* after it.

1 Rory carried his bag filled with many-coloured stockings.

2 He walked, wearily and slowly, along the lane.

3 The pretty cottage, with its grey roof and white walls, stood in a large garden.

4 The small room, warm and comfortable, was lit by the glow of the fire.

Clauses are small groups of words similar to **phrases**, except clauses contain a proper **verb**.
Examples: The old man stood up and spoke to Rory.

This sentence has two verbs and two clauses:
1 The old man *stood* up
2 and *spoke* to Rory.

B Write out the two clauses in each of these sentences, and neatly underline the verbs.

1 The knife and fork jumped up from the dresser and cut down a piece of meat.

2 Potatoes jumped into the bucket of water and washed themselves thoroughly.

3 When they had eaten their supper, Rory and the old man rose from the table.

4 Unless you tell a story you will have to go.

5 He walked off along the road and saw the glow of a fire.

6 Hold the spit and turn the meat.

7 I threw the meat from me, but it followed me.

Look
Cover
Remember
Write
Check

A Make a list of the words in the story, and shown in this picture, which have the **ckle** pattern.

Learn these words, and ask a friend to test you.

B **ckle** and **kle** patterns sound the same. Choose the correct pattern to finish each of these words. Check your answers using a dictionary.

1 ti ____   2 an ____   3 sprin ____

4 chu ____   5 wrin ____   6 fre ____

7 ran ____   8 cra ____   9 tri ____

QUIZ

Spoonerisms

Dr Spooner from Oxford University was famous for accidentally muddling the sounds from words in a phrase.
Example: He said – It's good to ride on a well-boiled icicle.

He meant – It's good to ride on a well-oiled bicycle.

Can you work out what these spoonerisms really mean?

1 Hey! You're occupewing my pie.

2 No I'm not, I was sewn into this sheet.

3 This is a pasty tickled pie.

4 I've made a new habbit rutch for my right wabbit.

Make up some spoonerisms for yourself.

Hostile desert

Deserts can be hostile and dangerous places, especially for those who are unfamiliar with them. Here is an extract from a British traveller's description of his first journey across part of the Sahara desert.

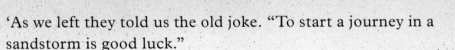

'As we left they told us the old joke. "To start a journey in a sandstorm is good luck."

'We camped the first night twenty miles south. The next morning we woke and came out of our tents at five. Too cold to sleep . . . Above us were the last stars. There would be no sunrise for another two hours. We passed around hot glasses of tea. The camels were being fed, half asleep, chewing the dates along with the date stones. We ate breakfast and then drank three more glasses of tea.

'Hours later we were in the sandstorm that hit us out of a clear morning, coming from nowhere. The breeze that had been refreshing had gradually strengthened. Eventually we looked down, and the surface of the desert was changed. Pass me the book . . . here. This is Hassanein Bey's wonderful account of such storms –

"It is as though the surface were underlaid with steam-pipes, with thousands of orifices through which tiny jets of steam are puffing out. The sand leaps in little spurts and whirls. Inch by inch the disturbance rises as the wind increases its force. It seems as though the whole surface of the desert were rising in obedience to some upthrusting force beneath. Larger pebbles strike against the shins, the knees, the thighs. The sand-grains

climb the body till it strikes the face and goes over the head. The sky is
shut out, all but the nearest objects fade from view, the universe is filled."

'We had to keep moving. If you pause sand builds up as it would
around anything stationary, and locks you in. You are lost forever.
A sandstorm can last five hours. Even when we were in trucks in
later years we would have to keep driving with no vision. The worst
terrors came at night. Once, north of Kufra, we were hit by a storm
in the darkness. Three a.m. The gale swept the tents from their
moorings and we rolled with them, taking in sand like a sinking boat
takes in water, weighed down, suffocating, till we were cut free by a
camel driver.

'We travelled through three storms during nine days. We missed
small desert towns where we expected to locate more supplies. The
horse vanished. Three camels died. For the last two days there was
no food, only tea . . . After the third night we gave up talking. All
that mattered was the fire and the minimal brown liquid.

'Only by luck did we stumble on the desert town of El Taj.'

From *The English Patient* by Michael Ondaatje.

A Copy and complete these sentences with one or more words.

1 They travelled ____ miles on the first day.

2 ____ was their main drink throughout the journey.

3 In a sandstorm it is important to ____ .

4 During the journey they lost ____ .

B Write sentences to answer these questions.

1 In which desert were they travelling?

2 What do you think the writer means by 'the universe is filled'?

3 Why were they particularly concerned about the nights?

4 What similarity does the writer suggest between being in a desert and being at sea? Can you think of any others?

VOCABULARY

Hyperbole

Hyperbole is exaggeration.
Example: I was so thirsty I could have drunk the river dry.

It can sometimes be fun to use **hyperbole,** but remember it really weakens your argument if you want your reader to take you seriously.

A Change these into less exaggerated statements.

1 When the sun went down I thought I would freeze to death.

2 I didn't close my eyes all night.

3 We could hear our drivers ranting and raving at each other.

4 We were drowned by the heavy rain.

B Choose an ordinary word from the box to match with each hyperbole (exaggeration).

angry	dreamy	confused	hungry	frightened

1 starving to death

2 too scared to breathe

3 doesn't know whether she's on her head or her heels

4 makes my blood boil

5 doesn't know what day it is

PUNCTUATION

Hyphens

Never split a word unless you really have to!

Remember, **hyphens** are used to join words to make compound adjectives.

Example: the near-exhausted camel driver

Hyphens can also be used to divide a word so that part of it is on one line and part on the next.

Example: Inch by inch the disturbance rises as the
wind increases in force.

Try to avoid splitting words at the end of a line, but if it is essential, say the word out loud and split it where it seems natural. If the word has double letters, place the hyphen between these letters. Neither part of the split word should ever have fewer than three letters. Do not split words with only one syllable.

Example: trotting *trot-ting*

A Divide these words as if they were to be split between two lines.

1	sandstorm	2	budding	3	regrettable	4	peculiarity
5	sadness	6	children	7	terrified	8	increasingly
9	craziness	10	changing	11	swimming	12	unfortunately

> Clauses have a proper verb; phrases don't.

Remember, a **clause** is a small group of words in a sentence. Each **clause** needs its own **verb**.
Example: <u>The sun was hot</u> so we wore our hats.

This sentence has two clauses. In sentences with two clauses, one of the clauses is usually more important and is called the **main clause**.

The sun was hot is the main clause.
The main clause can usually be a sentence by itself.

A Copy these sentences and use a ruler to underline the main clause in each.

1 We were going on a long journey so we took a good supply of food and water.

2 The worst time was at night when the cold winds blew.

3 We had excellent guides who knew all the dangers.

4 I can now ride camels well, though they make me feel seasick.

B Here are three main clauses and some conjunctions. Use the conjunctions in the box to add a second clause to each of the main clauses. You may be able to think of several clauses for each main clause. The first is done to help you.

and	so	although	because	after	before	when	but

> Try adding some clauses in front of the main clause.

The camels were powerful   **and** able to carry heavy loads.
The camels were powerful   **although** their legs looked thin and fragile.

Deserts are dangerous places

We eventually reached El Taj

The **main clause** does not have to come first.
Example: When we had travelled twenty miles **we made our first camp**.

C Copy these sentences and underline the main clause in each. Some main clauses are first and some are second.

1 As soon as I put my head down I was fast asleep.

2 Sand had got into everything by the time we completed our journey.

3 Exploring deserts is very exciting, though it can be dangerous.

4 Although we warned them against it, they set off despite the sandstorm forecast.

SPELLING

'ious' or 'ous'?

Look
Cover
Remember
Write
Check

Here are two groups of words that often cause problems, even for good spellers.
You simply need to learn and remember which of the words that end with the **ous** suffix also need an **i**.

delicious	ferocious	generous	
vicious	furious	enormous	
serious	previous	mischievous	
victorious	religious	marvellous	

A Cover the two groups of words, then write one word to go with each of these clues. Each answer must end with **ous**.

1 tasty

2 very angry

3 huge

4 winning

5 frighteningly aggressive

6 wonderful

7 solemn

8 having a religion

QUIZ
Word pyramid

Copy and complete this word pyramid. One new letter is introduced somewhere in each row to make each new word. The clues will help you.

1 another word for 'me'

2 antonym of 'out'

3 a bad or wrong action

4 to make music with your mouth

5 wasps do this

6 for tying parcels

7 chewy (meat)

Disaster in Bangladesh

Many major disasters are caused by hurricanes, and very many of the deaths from these devastating storms occur in Bangladesh. In one of the worst disasters recorded, 200,000 people died when a hurricane struck. The story of how that tragedy affected just one of the coastal islands helps to explain the problems that face the people there.

Bangladesh, which is situated in southern Asia immediately east of India, remains one of the poorest countries in the world, and many of its people are constantly close to starvation, and frequently threatened by the terrible storms that occur in this part of the world.

Most of Bangladesh is located on the low-lying land where the mighty Ganges and Brahmaputra rivers reach the sea. Together these great rivers create one of the biggest deltas in the world. As the rivers dump their silt in the sea the delta grows and grows; new islands appear every few days. As each new island is formed, poor people rush to claim part of the land to farm in order to supply food for their families. When these mudflats first appear they are not very fertile, and are very likely to be destroyed again by the sea. Nevertheless, peasant farmers build simple huts of bamboo, which they thatch with grass. They scratch a living as best they can by raising cattle on the poor, thin grass, and from rice which they grow in the small paddies.

Uri Char is scarcely an island; it might more accurately be described as a mudflat by the sea. In most parts of the world it would be uninhabited but, because the population of Bangladesh is growing so rapidly and as there is such pressure on available land for farming, islands like Uri Char are home to thousands of Bangladeshi people. About 2000 poor farmers and their families inhabit Uri Char knowing that they can be washed away in a storm at any time, but they have nowhere else to go. If they did not try to farm here they would probably starve, so they have little real choice!

One night, vicious winds lashed the islands and the sea boiled ferociously as another cyclone roared in from the Bay of Bengal. A huge wave of water, taller than a house, surged relentlessly at about 20 kilometres per hour towards the mudflat island. By the time the people realised their inevitable plight it was too late to escape. The seas were too rough for the people to flee to the mainland.

Here is the report from the *Daily Telegraph* journalist who visited the devastated area immediately after the storm.

Cyclone death toll 'may reach 40,000'

By MUFAZZAL HUSAIN in Dacca

Thousands of bodies are floating in the Bay of Bengal in the aftermath of the cyclone and 45ft tidal wave which hit the coast region of Bangladesh last Friday.

Three thousand bodies have been recovered so far, but unofficial estimates put the death toll at up to 40,000.

An official source in the district of Noakhali said 6,000 people were washed away into the Bay of Bengal.

Communications with the coastal areas and islands of the region are not yet fully restored but a spokesman at the disaster central headquarters in Dacca said at least 12,000 people were missing from seven islands which took the brunt of the tidal wave.

'Worst Tragedy'

President Ershad, who has cancelled a visit to China due to start today, described the wave as the "worst tragedy in Bangladesh's history".

About 250,000 people have lost their homes and President Ershad has mobilised the three armed services on a war footing to provide relief services.

Helicopters are dropping food and drinking water to survivors and navy ships are ploughing through rain and heavy seas to reach cut-off islands.

One report said hundreds of survivors on bamboo rafts and floating rooftops were being stalked by sharks and crocodiles as they awaited rescue.

A survivor said he spent 48 hours clinging to his wooden bed before a ship picked him up about 20 miles out to sea.

The Bangladesh Navy said a search ship, the Darshak, had picked up 100 bodies and rescued about 1,000 people from the sea near the island of Sandwip.

A 15 year-old girl described how she lost her parents, two brothers and a sister.

"We were all sleeping in the same hut, but when the cyclone came all the others vanished and I was jammed against a fallen tree," she said.

Rescue officials were concerned about the fate of 2,000 people living on the furthermost island of Uri Char, about 25 miles off Chittagong.

Navy and army teams scouring the island and surrounding seas have so far found no sign of life.

The full extent of the disaster is unlikely to be known until the ships reach several low-lying mud islands mainly populated by fishermen.

But the plight of the survivors is known to be desperate as the sea has washed away their food supplies, polluted their drinking water and ruined crops.

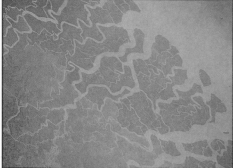

The Ganges Delta from space

What of the future?

The government of Bangladesh would like to help but it has serious problems. There is no spare land elsewhere for these poor farmers, and there is very little money to build sea defences. Weather stations broadcast warnings when cyclones are forecast, but few of the people own radios. Even if they could be warned, they are unlikely to be able to escape in time. Tragically, all this means that there are other similar disasters just waiting to happen.

COMPREHENSION

A Copy these sentences, filling in the gaps.

1 Bangladesh is east of ____ .

2 The great rivers ____ and ____ form a huge delta.

3 When the cyclones strike the islands of Bangladesh, the people have no way to ____ .

4 At first the newspaper reporter thought the death toll was ____ people, but afterwards we discovered it was ____ .

B Write sentences to answer these questions.

1 What is a delta?

2 Why do people live in such dangerous places as Uri Char?

3 What words are used to describe the conditions on the night of the tragedy?

4 What actions would you suggest to minimise the risk of such a terrible loss of life in the future?

VOCABULARY

Unnecessary words

Sometimes we use more words than we need, which can make our writing clumsy and less interesting for our reader.

Example: The reason why I believe that the cyclone caused so much loss of life was because I think that there were so many people living on the densely populated islands which were very crowded.

The cyclone caused so much loss of life because the islands were densely populated.

A How short a sentence can you write to include all the information in these sentences?

1 The real basic cause of the actual problem is that the country is really too poor to have the money to spend on housing all its people in areas where they could probably be safe and sound.

2 Unfortunately it is a shame and a pity that ever since so many people have been deciding to settle on the islands, there haven't been any protective dams built to shield them from the floods of water.

Some words include a 'sense of direction' in their meaning. When we use these words it is usually better to avoid adding *extra* prepositions.

Example: The mud covered *up* the young crops.
The mud covered the young crops.

B Cut out the unnecessary words in these sentences.

1 A small boat arrived there just in time.

2 The family descended down from the roof.

3 They agreed to cross over to the mainland.

4 As they left, they turned around to take a last look.

5 "We shall return back when the water subsides," promised their mother.

When writing to an organisation or company we use a slightly different layout than if we were writing a personal letter to a friend. Notice how all the paragraphs start at the left-hand side.

A **business letter** has seven parts.

Example:

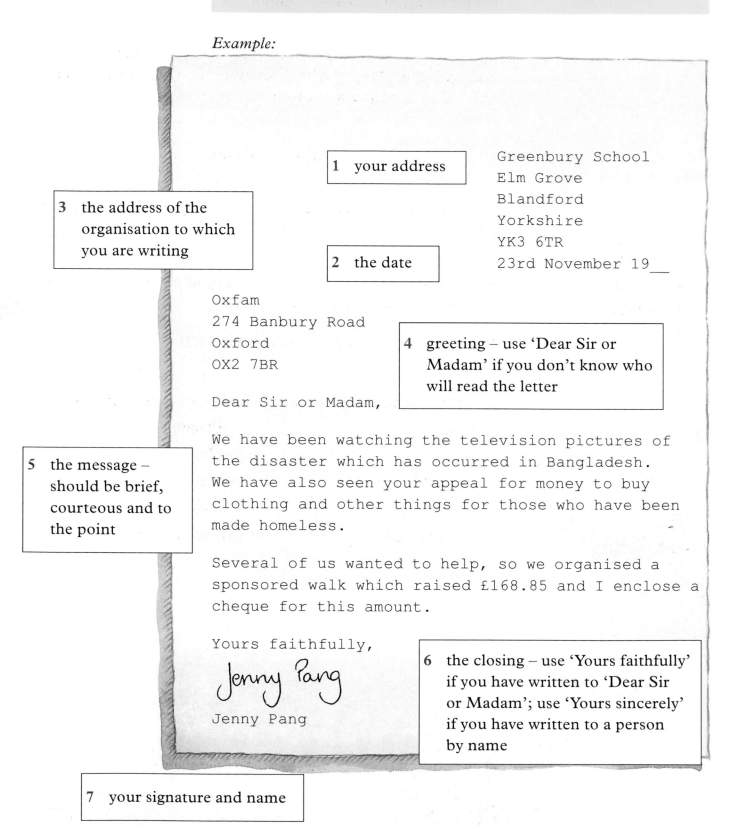

1	your address

```
Greenbury School
Elm Grove
Blandford
Yorkshire
YK3 6TR
23rd November 19__
```

2	the date

3	the address of the organisation to which you are writing

```
Oxfam
274 Banbury Road
Oxford
OX2 7BR

Dear Sir or Madam,
```

4	greeting – use 'Dear Sir or Madam' if you don't know who will read the letter

5	the message – should be brief, courteous and to the point

```
We have been watching the television pictures of
the disaster which has occurred in Bangladesh.
We have also seen your appeal for money to buy
clothing and other things for those who have been
made homeless.

Several of us wanted to help, so we organised a
sponsored walk which raised £168.85 and I enclose a
cheque for this amount.

Yours faithfully,

Jenny Pang

Jenny Pang
```

6	the closing – use 'Yours faithfully' if you have written to 'Dear Sir or Madam'; use 'Yours sincerely' if you have written to a person by name

7	your signature and name

Remember, layout and neatness are important.
Arrange your letter in the centre of your sheet of paper.
Allow a margin of at least 2 cm on each side.
Read your letter when you have finished. If you are not satisfied with any part of it, write it again.

A Write a business letter yourself. If there is something you want to know, or if there is something you want to say or suggest to an organisation, write a letter to them about it.

SPELLING

'augh' pattern

Same pattern, but not always the same sounds!

taught   caught   naughty   daughter   fraught
draught   haughty   laugh   taught

Their **daughter** became **fraught** when they were **caught** by the floods.

A Ask a friend to test you to see how many of these words you can learn to spell in five minutes.

B Write a short sentence for each of the words.

QUIZ

Bangladesh

Draw or trace a map of Bangladesh. On it mark these features.

1	Dhaka	2	Chittagong
3	Barisal	4	Khulna
5	Rajshahi	6	Mymensingh
7	Narayanganj	8	The Bay of Bengal
9	River Ganges	10	River Brahmaputra

Which countries border Bangladesh?

Check-up 3

A What do these proverbs mean?

1 More haste less speed.

2 When the cat's away the mice will play.

3 Two wrongs don't make a right.

B 1 What is an *interjection*?

2 Write a sentence which needs an interjection about an incident at the zoo.

C Write one or two words that could be used in place of the hyperbole in these sentences.

1 Looking down into the lions' enclosure, I felt <u>scared to death</u>.

2 By the time we stopped for lunch I <u>could have eaten a horse</u>.

3 In the afternoon it started to <u>rain cats and dogs</u>.

4 Our teacher said that when we mess about it <u>makes his blood boil</u>.

D Use your thesaurus or dictionary to find a synonym and an antonym for each of these words.

1 delicious	2 fierce	3 exciting
4 cruel	5 wild	6 lovely

E Rewrite this passage, omitting the unnecessary words, and making it more interesting for the reader.

When the day arrived when we were all due to go on our outing to visit the animals at the zoo, I felt really very highly excited. Mum said that when I sat on the coach it would be good if I could find a seat and sit next to one of my friends. When we had all climbed up on board the big enormous coach it drove through the gates out of our school. We all knew and said to each other that we thought we were going to have a really really good day at the zoo.

PUNCTUATION

A Neatly set out and write a business letter to the director of a zoo, or any other place you may have visited, describing something that particularly impressed you or something about which you were unhappy.

B Write this short passage, adding the capital letters and punctuation marks, and starting new lines where necessary.

i really hate spiders or thought i did until we went to the insect house does anyone here hate spiders enquired the keeper i put my hand up but immediately wished i hadnt come here and i will show you how gentle they are but i hate spiders i pleaded dont worry i wont force you to touch one if you are frightened in the end i even held a large one in my hand without worrying you see said the keeper in his calm and reassuring voice there really is nothing at all to be worried about it is all in your mind afterwards maggie exclaimed wow you were brave not really i explained there really is no reason to be afraid of most spiders

GRAMMAR

A Copy these sentences, neatly underlining the adjective phrase or the adverb phrase in each. Next to each, write which type of phrase you have underlined.

1 The lion, strong and muscular, prowled around its enclosure.

2 We ran, as fast as we could, to watch the penguins being fed.

3 Slowly and carefully, the keeper entered the gorilla's cage.

4 The huge animal, quiet and menacing, sat and watched him.

B What is the most important difference between a clause and a phrase?

C Copy these sentences, neatly underlining the *main* clause in each.

1 Mum gave me an enormous packed lunch, which I didn't manage to finish.

2 You aren't allowed to feed the animals, since they can become ill.

3 We had an excellent day at the zoo, arriving home tired but happy.

PLEASE DO NOT FEED THE ANIMALS

SPELLING

A Finish the words to complete these sentences.

1 A syn ____ is a Jewish place of worship.

2 Our team is at the top of the lea ____ .

3 I looked in the cat ____ for a present for Mum.

B Choose either **ckle** or **kle** to complete these words.

1 ti ____	2 wrin ____	3 chu ____
4 an ____	5 ran ____	6 sprin ____

C Choose either **ous** or **ious** to complete these words.

1 delic ____	2 enorm ____	3 marvell ____
4 ser ____	5 fur ____	6 gener ____